A Taste of culture

Foods of the Philippines

Barbara Sheen

KIDHAVEN PRESS

An imprint of Thomson Gale, a part of The Thomson Corporation

THOMSON
TM
GALE

Detroit • New York • San Francisco • San Diego • New Haven, Conn.

Picture Credits:

Cover: Robert Holmes/CORBIS
Melanie Acevedo/Getty Images, 46; © Paul Almasy/CORBIS, 54; Thomas Barwick/Getty Images, 38; © Catherine Carnow/CORBIS, 13, 25; © Bennett Dean; Eye Ubiquitous/CORBIS, 12; © Michael Freeman/CORBIS, 45 (inset), 47; Courtesy of Hazeline Gadia, 18, 26; Getty Images, 31 (lower right), 40; David Greedy/Getty Images, 49; © Rob Howard/CORBIS, 33; © Richard I'Anson/Lonely Planet Images, 52; © Sian Irvine/Getty Images, 11; Courtesy of Cecile Aquino, 28; © Lonely Planet Images, 6 (inset), 30, 32, 43; Courtesy of Charles Luison, 23; Photodisc, 8, 10, 31 (upper left), 35 (lower); © Photos.com, 14, 16, 22, 27, 35 (upper left); © Romeo Ranoco/Reuters/CORBIS, 8, 24; © Reuters/CORBIS, 6; Courtesy of Mavic Ricasata, 51; Suzanne Santillan, 5; © Albrecht G. Schaefer/CORBIS, 15; © Paul A. Souders/CORBIS, 20, 39; © Ubiquitos/CORBIS, 53; © Nik Wheeler/CORBIS, 37; © Michael S. Yamashita/CORBIS, 45; Courtesy of Jeanelyn Zozobrado, 21

For more information, contact
KidHaven Press
27500 Drake Rd.
Farmington Hills, MI 48331-3535
Or you can visit our Internet site at http://www.gale.com

LIBRARY OF CONGRESS CATALOGING-IN-PUBLICATION DATA
Sheen, Barbara. 　Foods of the Philippines / by Barbara Sheen. 　　p. cm. — (A taste of culture) 　Includes bibliographical references and index. 　ISBN 0-7377-3454-X (hard cover : alk. paper) 1. Cookery, Philippine—Juvenile literature. 2. Philippines—Social life and customs—Juvenile literature. I. Title. II. Series. 　TX724.5.P5S54 2006 　641.59599—dc22 　　　　　　　　　　　　　　　　　　　　　　　　　　　　　　　2005025526

Printed in the United States of America

Contents

Chapter 1
Abundant Ingredients   4

Chapter 2
Global Tastes   17

Chapter 3
Sweet Treats   29

Chapter 4
Foods for Celebrations   42

Metric Conversions   56

Notes   57

Glossary   59

For Further Exploration   61

Index   63

Abundant Ingredients

The Philippines consists of more than 7,000 islands located in the Pacific Ocean. Good weather, fine soil, and waterways teeming with life provide the Filipino people with an abundant food supply. Rice, coconuts, fish, and seafood are especially plentiful. Filipino cooks use these important ingredients in almost all their recipes.

Rice at Every Meal

Rice has been growing in the Philippines for thousands of years. Rice paddies carpet the islands in vibrant shades of green and gold. If laid end to end, ancient rice terraces still in use today would encircle half the world. They reach 4,920 feet (1,500m) up the sides of Filipino mountains.

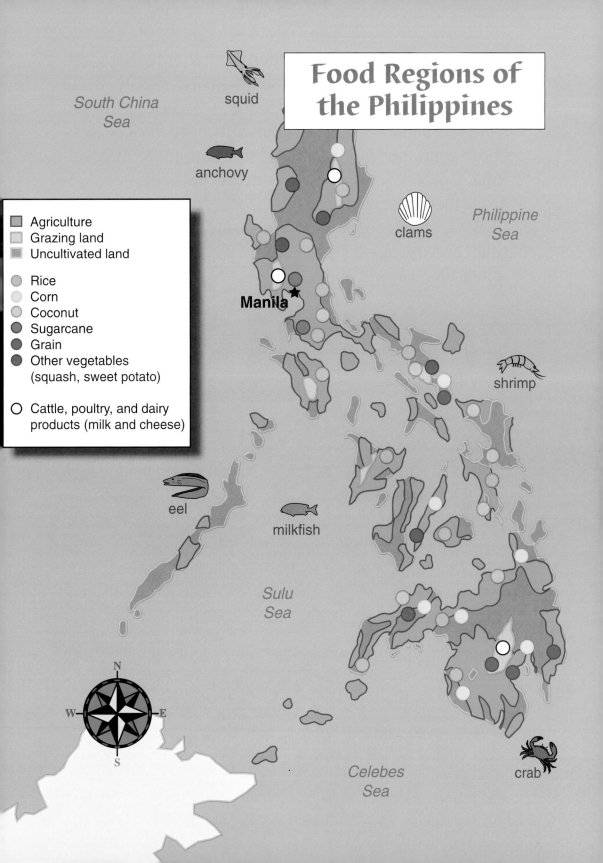

Dozens of different varieties of rice grow here. Filipinos use every kind in their cooking. Sticky white malagkit (ma-lahg-KIT), for example, is used to thicken stews, while sweet purple rice is a favorite in rice cakes. Short-grain, snow-white milagrosa is popular at mealtime. Golden rice, which is enriched with vitamin A, is also a mealtime choice.

Because it is so plentiful, and because Filipinos love its pure mild

Farmers carry rice stalks on their heads during the Philippines rice harvest, while bundled rice (inset) dries.

An Amazing Tree

The coconut palm may be the most useful tree in the world. One tree produces twelve different crops of nuts each year. The nuts provide millions of people with a rich source of protein. After all, one coconut has more protein than a large steak.

The juice inside the coconut is pure, sterile, and loaded with glucose, a natural sugar. During World War II, it was given to hospitalized patients to provide them with nutrition.

Coconut oil also has many uses. It is a common ingredient in shampoos, shaving creams, and skin lotions.

The tree itself is useful as well. In the past, the flowers were used to make shoes, caps, and helmets for soldiers. Even today the leaves are woven into clothing and furnishings. Coconut shells are often carved and used as platters. They are also ground up and used to make plastic. The roots are used to make mouthwash, as a treatment for stomach ailments, and as a dye.

taste, no meal is considered complete without rice. For breakfast, rice is fried with shrimp or sausage. It can also be steamed with coconut milk and cocoa to make a porridgelike dish called champorado. Fish and vegetables arranged around a large bowl of rice are popular for lunch and dinner. "Meals must include the staple rice," Manila journalist Millie Reyes explains, "or else a Filipino feels like he hasn't eaten at all."[1]

To make rice, Filipino cooks first rinse off the grains. Next, they place the rice in a pot of water, which they bring to a boil. Then, they lower the heat and let the rice simmer until the water is absorbed and the rice is soft and fluffy. Broth is often added to the cooked rice, which gives it a souplike consistency. This is known as arroz caldo.

Many Varieties and Uses

Not only do Filipinos eat rice with almost every meal, they use it to make flour, noodles, vinegar, dipping sauce, and wine. Immature rice grains are made into pinipig (pin-i-PIG), a substance similar to dried rice cereal. It adds crunch to many desserts and snacks. **Rice**

Huge yellow fin tuna, one of the many varieties of fish found in the waters of the Philippines, are headed for auction.

Champorado

This chocolate-flavored porridge is a favorite breakfast in the Philippines. For a richer, more exotic taste, cook the rice in a mix of half water, half coconut milk.

Ingredients:

1 cup uncooked white rice
4 cups water
$1/2$ cup unsweetened cocoa
$1/2$ cup sugar
$1/4$ teaspoon salt

Instructions:

1. Put the rice and water in a pot. Bring the water to a boil. Lower the heat and cover the pot. Let the rice simmer for about twenty minutes.
2. Mix the cocoa, sugar, and salt together. Pour the mixture over the rice, stirring well.
3. Cover the pot. Simmer the rice mixture for ten minutes more. Stir to keep the rice from sticking to the pot.
4. Serve in individual bowls with milk or coconut milk.
   Serves 4

washing, water that becomes rich with nutrients after rice is rinsed in it, is kept for use in stews and soups. Rice is so important to Filipinos that the International Rice Institute, the world's leading center for rice research, is headquartered here.

Fish and Seafood

Fish and seafood are other important parts of the Filipino diet. The islands are surrounded by the Pacific Ocean and dotted with rivers and lakes all bursting with edible water creatures. In addition human-made ponds are part of a thriving **aquaculture**, or fish-farming industry.

Filipinos eat fish and seafood morning, noon, and night. Sardines, octopus, squid, shrimp, catfish, snapper, bass, eel, clams, and sixteen different varieties of crabs all fill the pots of Filipino cooks. **Bangus** (bahn-GOOS), a mild-tasting whitefish also known as milkfish, thrives in rice paddies and ponds, and is a local favorite.

Filipino cooks have come up with many different ways to prepare fish and seafood. They steam and fry them and smoke them in banana leaves. They simmer them in black bean sauce, stew them in a vinegar–soy sauce known as **adobo** (a-DOH-boh), and boil them in **coconut milk**. They cook them in soups, salt them, dry them, and even eat them raw. Raw fish dishes are known as kinilaw (kin-EE-low). To prepare kinilaw, cooks marinate fresh fish or seafood in vinegar and lime juice. Acids in the marinade cook the fish without heat, changing the look and texture of the fish from pink to white just as heat does. At the same time, the marinade gives the ingredients a clean, sour taste.

Sinangag (Filipino Shrimp Fried Rice)

Filipinos use leftover rice to make this favorite dish. Beef, chicken, fish, sausage, or mixed vegetables can be substituted for the shrimp.

Ingredients:

2 tablespoons cooking oil
4 garlic cloves, cut into small pieces
1 celery stalk, cut into small pieces
1/2 small onion, cut into small pieces
4 cups cooked rice
1 cup cooked shrimp, cut into small pieces
1 tablespoon soy sauce

Instructions:

1. Heat the oil over medium heat in a large frying pan. Add the garlic, celery, and onion and fry, stirring frequently for about three minutes.
2. Add rice, shrimp, and soy sauce. Cook for about five minutes or until all the ingredients are hot. Stir frequently to prevent the rice from sticking.
   Serves 4

Coconuts are sliced open at harvest time. Coconut milk is used in many dishes.

Vinegar is a key ingredient in pakisaw (pahk-i-SOW), a cooking method in which fish and seafood are boiled in vinegar that has been flavored with ginger and pepper. Inihaw (in-EE-how), grilling whole fish over hot coals, is another delicious cooking technique.

Fish Sauces and Pastes

Filipino cooks also use fish and seafood as seasonings. They layer fish such as anchovies or shrimp with salt in clay pots. In a few months, the mixture forms a salty sauce and paste. The sauce is known as **patis** (pah-TEES), and the paste is called **bagoong** (bah-GOH-UN).

A vendor barbecues fish on a busy city street.

Filipinos first started making patis and bagoong hundreds of years ago as a way to preserve fish. Today they use the paste and sauce much as Westerners use salt. They also combine them with ingredients such as hot peppers, lime, and garlic to make a variety of dipping sauces known as **sawsawan** (sow-SOW-un). These sauces are served on tiny plates with almost every meal. Bagoong accompanies most meals, too. Chef Gilda

Cordero-Fernando explains that for Filipinos, "A major crime . . . is to be caught without ba-goong. Without bagoong, how can the . . . housewife even cook lunch?"[2]

The Tree of Life

Coconuts are another impor-tant part of the Filipino diet. Used in both foods and drinks, this delicious nut provides Filipinos with a rich source of protein, calcium, and vitamin B.

Coconuts have been growing in the Philippines for about 30,000 years. Experts believe the nuts originated in Indonesia and the ocean carried them to the Philippines. Over time the wind probably buried them with blowing sand, and they took root. A Filipino legend tells a more interesting tale, however. Supposedly an old man with bad eyesight found a coconut and thought it was a hu-man skull. He buried it, planting the first coconut palm in the Philippines.

Today more than 3 million coconut palms grow in the Philippines, making it the world's largest producer of co-conuts. Growing and selling the nuts provides one-quarter of the Philippine's people with jobs. That may be why Fili-pinos call the coconut palm "the tree of life."

Filipino cooks have hundreds of uses for coconuts. **Coconut juice** is a favorite thirst quencher. This sweet, clear liquid is found in the center of coconuts. Filipinos cut the nuts open and drink the juice right from the shell.

Exotic Fruits

Many delicious tropical fruits grow in the Philippines. Filipino cooks love to use them in their cooking. Fruit was once considered so valuable that it was a serious crime to pluck even one fruit off someone else's tree.

Among the most popular fruits are sweet ripe mangos. They are a main ingredient in fruit salads. Mango ice cream is a favorite treat. Green mangos, which are hard and sour, are also popular. Filipinos dip slices of the fruit in bagoong.

Other favorites include tamarind and jackfruit. Tamarind, a sour fruit, is used to add tartness to soups and stews. Jackfruit, which is the largest fruit in the world, reaching up to 100 pounds (45.36kg), is made into preserves or eaten fresh. It tastes a little like a banana. Its seeds are boiled and sprinkled with sugar. Unripe jackfruit is stewed in coconut milk with meat.

Brightly colored fruit attracts shoppers in the Philippines.

They also use it to make a thick gelatin that is popular in fruit salads.

For desserts and yummy snacks, Filipinos scoop out the snow-white nutmeat from fresh, young coconuts. This meat is soft and custardy, while that of mature nuts is crunchy. It adds chewy sweetness to candies, pies, fruit salads, and rice cakes. When it is grated, mixed with water, and squeezed through a cloth, the result is coconut milk.

Coconuts for Everyone

Filipinos use coconut milk in a number of ways. it is used instead of cow's milk in baking. They cook seafood, fish, chicken, meat, or vegetables in it to make a dish called **ginataan** (gin-AH-TAN). The coconut milk adds a delicious sweet flavor that Filipinos love. That may be why, according to Cordero-Fernando, "Twice or even thrice a day, the . . . table has some dish cooked in coconut milk, some-times two in a meal."[3]

With coconut palms grow-ing all over the islands, there are plenty of coconuts for every-one. Add to that acres of rice paddies and waterways teem-ing with life, and it becomes clear that the Philippines is blessed with a plentiful supply of their favorite ingredients.

chapter

2

Global Tastes

Filipino cooking is an interesting combination of foods from many different cultures. China, Japan, Spain, Malaysia, Mexico, the United States, and many others have influenced Filipino cooking. At one time or another the Philippines traded with, or was governed or occupied by, each of these nations. Favorite dishes, such as adobo, **pancit** (pahn-SIT), and **sinigang** (sin i-GAH-UN), reflect these different influences, but with unique Filipino touches. Of course there are regional differences throughout the Philippines. For example, residents of the southern island of Mindanao like to add hot chile to their cooking, and because many Mindanaoins are Muslim, they do not eat pork for religious reasons. Residents of the northern island of Luzon, on the other hand, often

A plate of chicken adobo with rice makes a wonderful picnic meal.

add bits of pork to vegetable dishes to give them extra flavor. Central islanders prefer dried and salted fish dishes and sugar-coated fruit dishes. Despite these differences, however, adobo, pancit, and sinigang are popular throughout the islands.

The National Dish

Adobo is frequently called the national dish of the Philippines. It is both a tangy sauce and the basis for a rich, hearty stew of chunks of chicken, meat, fish, seafood, or vegetables.

Filipinos first tasted adobo during the sixteenth century when the Spanish brought their version to the Philippines. It was made with olive oil, garlic, oregano, and vinegar. The vinegar acted as a preservative, which was one reason why adobo quickly became popular in the hot Philippines, where food spoils quickly. Filipino cooks substituted native rice vinegar or coconut palm vinegar for the Spanish wine vinegar used. They replaced the olive oil and oregano, which were not readily available, with pepper and ginger. They also added soy sauce, which they got centuries earlier from the Chinese. In the process, they created a tart, salty, savory dish that is uniquely Filipino.

Most anything can be stewed in adobo sauce. Chicken, pork, beef, frogs' legs, seafood, fish, green beans, and eggplants all go well with it. Filipinos have even been known to use crickets and, in a salute to American influence, to add cola to the sauce. Because whatever ingredients a cook has on hand can be turned into adobo,

A family enjoys Sunday lunch near their market stall in the capital city of Manila.

and because Filipinos love its tart, hearty flavor, a pot of the rich stew can be found bubbling in almost every Filipino kitchen. Journalist Olivia Wu describes the kitchen of a Filipino grandmother she visited: "At her house . . . her rice cooker sits on [warm] mode 24 hours a day, and an adobo is always curling up steam that is pungent with earthy, vinegary aromas."[4]

Chicken adobo is among the most popular choices. To make this delicious dish, cooks marinate the chicken in adobo sauce, which is comprised of vinegar, soy sauce,

Chicken Adobo

Adobo is not difficult to make. It is usually served with rice. Since the sauce contains vinegar, use a large nonaluminum saucepan such as enamel, cast iron, or stainless steel. Aluminum interacts with vinegar, changing the taste.

Ingredients:

1 chicken cut into 4 to 6 pieces
$1/2$ onion, chopped
2 garlic cloves, minced
$1/2$ cup white vinegar or apple cider vinegar
$1/2$ teaspoon pepper
1 bay leaf
4 tablespoons soy sauce
$1/2$ cup water
2 tablespoons vegetable oil

Instructions:

1. Put the oil in a large saucepan. Brown the chicken with the onion and garlic.
2. Add the remaining ingredients. Let the mixture come to a boil.
3. Lower the heat. Let the mixture simmer until the chicken is thoroughly cooked, about 35 minutes. Remove the bay leaf before serving.
   Serves 4

garlic, pepper, and ginger. Next, they fry the chicken until it is lightly browned. Finally, they place the fried chicken in a stew pot, and pour more marinade over it. The mixture is slowly simmered until the sauce thickens and the flavors blend together. Coconut milk is often added to the simmering adobo. This gives it a sweet flavor and an exotic fragrance. Filipino chef Gene Gonzalez explains: "The miracle of flavors happens when a few pieces of chopped garlic infuses with spritzes of vinegar, and blends with the other ingredients producing a truly appetizing, yet simple and economical, dish."[5]

Adobo is usually served with rice. Many cooks do not serve it immediately, but instead refrigerate it overnight. This gives the ingredients a chance to blend. Reheating the adobo the next day thickens the sauce, making it even more flavorful. When it is finally served, the taste is irresistible.

Pancit's International Flavors

Pancit, which is a general term for any noodle dish, is another Filipino favorite with international roots. The Chinese brought noodles to the Philippines in the ninth century. Modern Filipino cooks use Chinese rice, egg, and bean thread noodles, which are thin white noodles made from

Egg Noodle Pancit

This pancit dish calls for egg or ramen noodles. Angel hair pasta or vermicelli will also work well. Cooked shrimp or pork can be substituted for the chicken.

Ingredients:

1 package (8 ounces) egg noodles or ramen
1 onion, chopped
2 garlic cloves, chopped
1 celery stalk, chopped
1 pound cooked chicken, cut into small pieces
1 cup chicken broth
pinch black pepper
1 tablespoon soy sauce
2 tablespoons vegetable oil

Instructions:

1. Cook the noodles according to the package directions.
2. Heat some vegetable oil in a pan over medium heat. Brown the onion and garlic. Add the celery, chicken, and cooked noodles.
3. In a medium bowl, mix together the broth, pepper, and soy sauce. Pour it over the noodles.
4. Cover the pan and let the mixture simmer on a low heat for five minutes or until most of the broth is absorbed.
   Serves 4

A worker checks on rice noodles, sometimes used in pancit, drying in the sun.

mashed mung beans, to make pancit. They may also use Japanese wheat noodles.

The noodles are mixed with a variety of ingredients. Pancit may contain tiny shrimp, which are still alive when added to the pot. It also may include beef, pork, sausage, chicken, or chicharon, which is fried pig skin. Vegetables, such as carrots, celery, and onions, and mushrooms add color and flavor. Fried garlic, which the Spanish introduced to the Philippines in the sixteenth century, provides a mouthwatering scent.

Since each noodle has a different taste and texture, Filipino cooks match noodles to the ingredients that complement them. For instance, rice, bean thread, and egg noodles are light and delicate. Cooks combine these with other delicate-tasting foods such as shrimp and chicken. Wheat noodles are thick and hearty. Filipino cooks match them with beef, pork, and sausage.

Uniquely Filipino Sauce

No matter the ingredients, one thing makes pancit different from the noodle dishes of other countries: the sauce that tops it. Filipino cooks make a number of different sauces for pancit. The sauce may be as simple as chicken broth flavored with soy sauce. It may contain broth, bagoong, egg yolks, and the juice of kalamansi limes. These tiny limes have green, yellow, or orange skin; bright orange flesh; and an extremely sour taste. Sometimes a liquid made from annatto seeds—a spice that originated in Mexico and was brought by the Spanish to the Philippines—is added to the sauce. This turns the sauce a bright red and gives it a sweet, spicy flavor.

Patrons enjoy eating and drinking at a roadside noodle stand.

A Different Way of Eating

Unlike many of their Asian neighbors, Filipinos do not use chopsticks. In the past Filipinos ate with their hands. They would form rice into small balls with their fingers. Then, they would roll small pieces of meat, fish, and vegetables into the rice ball. Finally, they carried the rice ball to their mouths with their fingertips.

Although some modern Filipinos still eat with their hands, most use a fork and spoon. Diners hold the fork in their left hand and the spoon in their right. They use the fork like a spear and the spoon like a knife. Once they have torn the food with the spoon, diners use the fork to push the food onto the spoon, which is used to carry the food to the mouth.

Rather than use chopsticks, most Filipino children eat with a fork and spoon.

With or without annatto seeds, pancit sauces are delicious. When the sauce is poured over noodles, the tastes of other cultures combine with Filipino flavors to form a new and delicious creation. Chef Gerry Gelle says that pancit is "a truly international dish: the rice noodles are Chinese, the garnish is native Filipino dried fish, and the sauce is made with annatto which has it roots in Mexican cooking."[6]

Sour Soup

Sinigang, a tart soup, is another favorite Filipino food with global origins. Experts believe that ancient Malaysian settlers brought it to the Philippines in the form of chicken broth flavored with fish sauce and fruits such as limes or lemongrass. Filipino cooks changed the broth by making it from rice washing. This gave it a flavor like rice. They also added shrimp, beef, or pork chops to the soup, as well as tomatoes, radishes, onions, and greens. Whole bangus—head and all—is also popular. In fact, Filipinos insist that the head is the best-tasting part of this fish.

Patis and sour fruit juice flavor the soup. A wide variety of sour fruits such as kalamansi limes, lemons, green tomatoes, unripened guavas, pineapples, and tamarind can be used. Each adds a slightly different flavor and aroma. "If this Saturday the souring fruit used for the sinigang was tamarind," Cordero-Fernando recalls, "the next

Sinigang with whole fish heads is a popular soup in the Philippines.

Saturday it was soured with guavas. . . . Still another Saturday, it was fresh sour pineapples in the dish, but it still was sinigang."[7]

Unlike in the West, where soup is usually served at the start of the meal, sinigang is served along with the main dishes. Although the soup is served hot, its sharp, bracing flavor is quite refreshing on hot days. Since almost every day in the Philippines is quite warm, this makes sinigang a perfect dish for Filipinos.

Filipino cooks have managed to alter the soups to suit their taste and environment. They have done the same with Chinese and Japanese noodles and Spanish adobo. By adding ingredients and flavors that are distinctively Filipino, these international dishes have become national favorites.

chapter

3

Sweet Treats

Filipinos love sweets. Sugar cane has been growing in the Philippines for centuries. Historians even think that the Filipinos were the first people to use sugar in their cooking.

Today, sugary desserts are an important part of lunch and dinner. Sweet treats are also a favorite for **merienda** (merry-EN-dah), mid-morning and mid-afternoon snacks. Among everyone's favorites are a variety of banana treats, fruit-filled **halo-halo** (HAH-lo-HAH-lo), and sweet custardy **flan** (flahn).

Banana Treats

Filipinos have been eating bananas for centuries. Many experts think the first wild bananas, which were only

A smiling shopkeeper welcomes customers to her shop filled with sweets and refreshing drinks.

about the size of a man's finger, originated in the Philippines. Today twenty different varieties grow here. There are red-skinned morados, teeny señoritas, and long, yellow Cavendish bananas, all of which can be peeled and eaten once they ripen.

Fat and hard **sabas** (sah-BAHS), on the other hand, need to be cooked before they can be eaten. Once cooked, they are quite tasty. This makes them perfect for a wide range of cooked banana treats that Filipinos love. For instance, sabas are ideal for banana cue, which is fire-roasted banana on a stick. To make this popular treat, sabas are peeled, skewered onto bamboo sticks, roasted over hot charcoal, then rolled in brown sugar. Street vendors throughout the Philippines sell this yummy treat and hungry Filipinos can often be seen walking through the streets nibbling on banana cue.

Baked Bananas

Baked bananas are a popular Filipino snack. In this recipe the bananas are sprinkled with sugar. They can also be sprinkled with grated coconut, cinnamon, or honey. Baked bananas taste good alone, but they also taste great spooned on top of ice cream.

Ingredients:

4 ripe bananas
2 tablespoons melted butter
1/4 cup sugar

Instructions:

1. Preheat the oven to 375°F.
2. Spray a baking pan with cooking spray.
3. Peel the bananas. Cut them into 1/4-inch rounds.
4. Place the banana rounds in the baking pan. Brush the tops with melted butter and sprinkle with sugar.
5. Bake for fifteen minutes.

Serves 4

Bananas, pineapples, and other delicious fruits are used in Filipino desserts.

Sabas are also used to make banana chips. Filipinos eat these sweet chips the way Americans eat potato chips. To make them, cooks peel the bananas and cut them into round slices. Then they roll the slices in sugar and fry them until they are crisp and golden brown. Once

A banana seller carries his produce to sell to villagers in the northern region of Luzon.

the chips cool, they are stored in airtight containers, which keep them crunchy.

Pounded bananas are another favorite saba treat. This dish begins with boiled bananas that are mixed with brown sugar and grated coconut. The mix is pounded into a sticky paste and rolled into little balls that are soft, sweet, and delicious. A Filipino woman recalls: "Many days when my brother and I got home from school binayong saging [pounded banana] was waiting for us on the table. It's . . . a good filling snack."[8]

Besides being a good snack, banana treats are surprisingly nutritious. Bananas are loaded with potassium and other vital nutrients. They also contain tryptophan, a type of protein that makes people feel relaxed and happy. It is no wonder that they are a Filipino favorite.

The Queen of Desserts

Bananas are also a popular ingredient in halo-halo, a fruit dish that is known in the Philippines as "the queen of desserts." Halo-halo, which means "mix-mix," is a delightful combination of any number of ingredients such as sweet, juicy tropical fruits; coconut; gelatin; sweet beans; shaved ice; evaporated milk; ice cream; and jelly. It is, according to chef Reynaldo Alejandro, "the Philippine's most beloved treat. . . . It features exotic fruits and sweets that Filipinos enjoy."[9]

Exactly what goes into halo-halo depends on the cook's taste and imagination. A typical halo-halo begins with a scoop of shaved ice in a tall dessert glass. Layer upon layer of fruit, such as shredded melon, cubed ripe

Halo-Halo

Halo-halo can contain almost any fruit. This recipe is only one of many possible combinations. Feel free to use your imagination.

Ingredients:

4 tablespoons shaved ice
4 teaspoons mango, cut into small cubes
4 teaspoons pineapple, cut into small cubes
4 teaspoons honeydew melon, cut into small cubes
4 teaspoons bananas, cut into rounds
4 teaspoons shredded coconut
4 tablespoons evaporated milk
4 scoops vanilla ice cream

Instructions:

1. Divide the shaved ice between four tall dessert glasses.
2. On top of the ice, layer the fruits and coconut in any order.
3. Pour one tablespoon of evaporated milk over the top of each mixture. Top with a scoop of ice cream.
4. Serve with long spoons so diners can mix the ingredients. Serves 4

mango, mashed bananas, and fresh pineapple chunks top the ice. Mashed sweet potato, beans cooked in sticky syrup, purple yam jelly, and shredded coconut often follow. The whole thing is topped with a delicious splash of sweet evaporated milk, coconut milk, or a scoop of ice cream. Some people use all three. Finally, it is crowned with a sprinkle of crisp pinipig. Diners halo, or mix, the ingredients together with a long spoon. They hurry to eat the concoction before the ice melts, as it tastes best while the layer of ice is still crunchy.

Halo-halo

Halo-halo tastes like a cross between an ice-cream sundae and a rich fruit salad. It is sweet, crunchy, creamy, and juicy all at the same time. It is the perfect treat on a steamy summer's day. That may be why roadside stands selling halo-halo to hungry passersby spring up all over the islands during the summer. Buyers can choose from about ten different ingredients. Then they watch as the vendor prepares the dish right before their eyes. Cordero-Fernando describes a typical halo-halo stand in this way: "On summer, a rough kitchen table is often pulled out to the road, under a tree or a thatched-roofed shed. A block of ice, wrapped in a burlap sack, makes its appearance together with a manual ice scraper and ten rows of jars with components."[10]

Once the mixture is complete, customers sit down on benches set out under palm trees and savor the delicious treat. Its icy freshness makes it hard to resist.

School children enjoy ice cream cones on a steamy afternoon.

Luscious Flan

Flan, a type of custard, is bathed in a caramel glaze.

Flan, a sweet milk and egg custard, is another luscious treat. The Spanish brought it to the Philippines in the 1500s. To make flan, cooks boil sugar and water together until the mixture turns into golden caramel syrup. Then, they pour the syrup into the bottom of oval flan molds, which are known as lyaneras in the Philippines. These can be just big enough for a single serving, or they can be the size of a small pie pan. Cooks then pour a custard mix of egg yolks, whole milk, sugar, and vanilla over the caramel.

The lyanera is placed in what is known as a bain marie or **water bath**. That is, the lyanera is placed into a larger pan filled with about 1 inch (2.54cm) of hot water. The whole thing is placed inside the oven to bake or on the stove top to steam. The flan is done when the custard is set.

The water bath protects the flan from direct heat, which can cause proteins in the eggs to harden and get crusty. Instead the egg mix becomes moist, soft, rich, and velvety.

After the flan cools, the cook inverts it onto a plate, and the carmel tops the flan like amber icing. Because cooks use egg yolks rather than whole eggs, this flan has a much creamier taste than flan that is made with whole eggs.

Filipino Fast Food

Roadside stands, bus stations, and shopping malls offer hungry Filipinos their own version of fast food. These stands are known as turo-turo, or point-point, because customers do not have to speak. They just point to the food they want.

The food is displayed on the front counter. When customers point to their selections, their choice is served immediately by agile waitresses who can handle ten or more orders at one time. Common choices include adobo, fried chicken, pancit, fish cooked in coconut milk, and hard-boiled eggs.

A woman prepares grilled chicken strips at a food stand.

A Filipino woman carries a tray of delicious cake.

The practice of using egg yolks rather than whole eggs to make flan is distinctly Filipino. According to Filipino legend, cooks got the egg yolks from Spanish priests who used egg whites to seal up cracks in the walls of their churches. They could not use egg yolks for this purpose, so the priests threw them away. Hating to see the yolks go to waste, thrifty Filipino cooks used two egg yolks in place of each whole egg to make flan. As a result, their flan often contains as many as twelve egg yolks. Add to this the coconut milk that many Filipinos substitute for whole milk, and the bits of tropical fruit and shredded coconut that they often add to the mix, and what you have is a sweet tropical treat that almost everyone loves. Former Philippines resident and storyteller Dianne de Las Casas agrees. In an article on her Web site she explains: "Flan is one of my favorite desserts. My mother made this delicious egg custard for us when my brother and I were growing up. It's rich and decadent and always brings back sweet childhood memories."[11] Today, she makes flan for her own daughter.

Flan's creamy taste is hard to resist, as is the exotic flavor of halo-halo and the luscious tastes of banana treats. It is no wonder that these delicious delicacies are so popular.

Foods for Celebrations

Filipinos love to celebrate. "By nature Filipinos are social and gregarious, eager to share their selves—and their food—with family and friends. . . . Any event will do to gather company and top the affair with food!"[12] explains Reyes. To make the event more fun, special foods such as **lechon** (LECH ohn), **lumpia** (LUM pia), and **bibingka** (bi BING kah) are likely to be served.

The Centerpiece of the Celebration

The centerpiece of many celebrations is lechon, a whole roasted baby pig. Birthdays, weddings, anniversaries, family reunions, and religious holidays nearly always include

To celebrate the harvest, a young woman dons an ornate costume made of rice.

lechon. People in the Filipino town of Balayan, for example, celebrate the birthday of Saint John the Baptist every June with a giant fiesta at which dozens of roasted pigs are served. Prominent townspeople provide the pigs. They are carried on long poles to the center of town, where tables are set up for everyone to feast.

Piglets, whose meat is more tender than that of older pigs, are used to make lechon. The customary way to prepare lechon is to roast the pig in a pit. To do this, cooks place charcoal in a pit dug in the ground. As the charcoal heats up, the pig, which is gutted by a butcher but is otherwise cooked whole, is marinated in vinegar. This tenderizes the meat. Next, the pig is stuffed with a wide range of ingredients. Banana leaves are one popular stuffing. The leaves are not eaten, but help the pig to cook evenly. As a result, the meat does not dry out but is instead moist and juicy.

Some cooks prefer edible stuffing such as brown rice, which picks up the flavor of the pig as it cooks inside. For the most festive occasions, a whole chicken may be stuffed inside the pig.

Pit Cooking

Once the pig has been stuffed, it is wrapped in banana leaves and placed in the hot pit. There it is buried under hot ashes. It can take all day for a pig to cook. When it is done, the skin is crisp and the meat is as soft as butter.

Lechon is usually served on a large platter, head and all. A sweet dipping sauce, made with the pig's liver and aptly named lechon sauce, always accompanies it. To make the sauce, the cook grinds the pig's liver into a paste and then fries it with garlic, onions, vinegar, sugar, salt, pepper, and bread crumbs.

Lechon has been served at Filipino feasts for centuries. Experts at Lutongbahay, a Web site dedicated to Filipino culture, explain: "An occasion would not be complete without the Lechon, or roasted pig. . . . It symbolizes the very heart of Filipino culture."[13]

Crisp, roasted pigs (inset) are sliced (below) and readied for hungry diners at a Manila restaurant.

Pork Ribs

Instead of making lechon for a party, busy Filipino cooks often serve pork ribs. This recipes calls for barbecuing the ribs. They also can be cooked for one hour in a 350°F oven.

Ingredients:

1/4 cup soy sauce
2 tablespoons lime juice
1/4 cup sugar
1 teaspoon salt
2 pounds pork ribs

Instructions:

1. Mix all the ingredients together, except the pork ribs. In a glass bowl or sealable plastic bag, pour the mixture over the ribs. Marinate the pork ribs in the mixture in the refrigerator overnight.
2. Spray a cool grill rack with cooking spray. Ask an adult to light the grill. Let the grill heat up.
3. Place the ribs on the grill rack. Cook until the ribs are thoroughly cooked, about 15 minutes. Turn them after 8 minutes.

Serves 4

Worth the Effort

Lumpia, or Filipino egg rolls, are another festive treat. These little cylindrical rolls are filled with a wide range of cooked meats, seafood, and vegetables. The filling is stuffed in a thin, light wrapper made from flour and egg yolks. Once stuffed, a lumpia can be served immediately. When eaten this way, it tastes fresh and soft. The lumpia may also be fried until the wrapper is crispy.

Hours of Work

Lumpia wrappers can be homemade, but many Filipino cooks buy ready-made wrappers to save time. This is because it takes a lot of time to make lumpia. Preparing the ingredients to fill the wrappers and then rolling them up can take hours. The ingredients must be finely chopped and cooked until tender. One lumpia can contain at least a half-dozen different ingredients. For instance, pork lumpia are filled with a mixture of ground pork, minced shrimp, potatoes, cabbage, garlic, green beans, jicama (a crunchy tropical vegetable), bagoong, and pepper. Other popular varieties contain any or all the previous ingredients plus others, such as ground beef, bangus, crabmeat, sausage, green papaya, raisins, and mushrooms, to name just a few possibilities. Although preparing all these ingredients is not easy, the mouthwatering aroma they produce as they cook makes

A plate of meat-filled lumpias makes a tasty treat.

the effort worthwhile. Chef Gerry Gelle explains: "If heaven were to have a smell, I would think it would smell like lumpia."[14]

Once the ingredients are ready, the cook places a spoonful in the corner of the wrapper. Then he or she carefully rolls the wrapper up to form a cylinder and seals the edges with water or egg. The lumpia can be served fresh, or it can be fried until it turns golden brown. Dozens of different dipping sauces are served with lumpia. Patis; peanut sauce, which tastes like peanut butter; and spicy chile–lime sauce are tasty choices.

It is not unusual for cooks to serve six or seven different varieties of lumpia and just as many sauces. Rolling lumpia takes hours. That is why many people hold lumpia-wrapping parties before the celebration. Friends and family members get together and roll lumpias as they visit with each other. Gelle recalls: "The family would gather and the tedious task of wrapping the lumpia was lightened with conversation, gossip, and an occasional song."[15]

A Christmas Treat

In addition to enjoying festive foods on special occasions, most Filipinos celebrate Christmas and prepare special foods for the holiday. Among the most popular Christmas treats is a flat cake called bibingka. For Filipinos, Christmas would not be the same without it.

Bibingka has an interesting taste. It combines sweet, salty, and sharp flavors. It can be made with wheat or rice

A Special Kettle

When Filipinos cook food for big fiestas, they often use a taliyasi (tal-EE-si). This deep cast-iron kettle, which can hold as much as 35 quarts (33.12l), is too big to fit in an oven. It is perfect for outdoor cooking.

Because not everyone owns a taliyasi, or even has room to store one, taliyasi owners gladly loan the pots to whoever needs one. The taliyasi is always returned with a package of food inside. When the owner of the kettle dies, it is inherited by his or her favorite person.

Pork simmers outdoors in a huge cast-iron kettle. This traditional meal is prepared for a Filipino festival.

flour. Rice flour gives bibingka a delicate taste, while wheat flour imparts a heartier taste. The choice is up to the baker.

To make bibingka, bakers make a batter of flour, sugar, eggs, butter, and coconut milk. They pour the batter into a cake pan lined with banana leaves. The leaves prevent the batter from sticking to the pan and give the cake a banana-like fragrance. When the cake is almost done, the baker sprinkles grated cheddar cheese over the top.

Bibingka

Bibingka is not hard to make. Instead of lining the baking pan with banana leaves, this recipe calls for waxed paper. Bibingka can also be baked directly in a greased baking pan.

Ingredients:
waxed paper
3 eggs, beaten
3/4 cup of sugar
1 1/4 cups coconut milk
2 teaspoons baking powder
1 teaspoon salt
4 tablespoons each: melted butter, shredded cheddar cheese, grated coconut
2 cups flour

Instructions
1. Preheat the oven to 375°F.
2. Spray a rectangular baking pan with cooking spray. Line the bottom of the pan with waxed paper and spray with cooking spray.
3. In a large bowl, mix together the eggs, sugar, and coconut milk. Add the baking powder, salt, two tablespoons of melted butter, and flour. Mix well.

Once the cheese melts, the cake is done. It is not quite ready for serving yet, though. A pat of butter; sugar; grated coconut; and sliced, salted hard-boiled eggs are scattered over the top. This gives the cake a sweet and salty taste that Filipinos love.

Filipinos have been eating bibingka at Christmas for hundreds of years. In the past, the cake was baked in a clay pot lined with banana leaves and placed directly into

4. Pour the mixture into the baking pan. Bake for 15 minutes.
5. Sprinkle the shredded cheese over the top of the bibingka and bake for 10 more minutes.
6. Pour the rest of the melted butter over the top of the bibingka. Sprinkle with the coconut.

Serve the cake warm.

Serves 6

Tasty Decorations

Residents of the town of Lukban, located on the northern Filipino island of Luzon, have an interesting way of celebrating the birth of Saint Isidro Labrador. They believe the saint was once a farmer in their town. Because he was such a good man, an angel helped him to plow his fields. Today, he is honored with a fiesta in which food is not only eaten, it is displayed everywhere.

People all over the island decorate the outside of their houses with rice leaves. Some people also add foods that represent the resident's occupation. For instance, vegetable farmers hang vegetables from their roofs and windows. Bakers hang cookies and butchers display strings of sausage.

Leaf-shaped rice wafers and various fruits and vegetables adorn this Luzon house.

A young Filipino girl carries a tray of cakes to villagers in Boracay Island in the central Philippines.

a charcoal fire. The cheese was made from the milk of water buffalo, animals found on many Filipino farms. Today, Filipino bakers use modern cake pans, gas or electric ovens, and prepackaged cheddar cheese. The tradition of eating bibingka at Christmas has not changed, however. Minette, a Filipino woman, explains: "When Christmas rolls around, visions of bibingka start dancing in my

Pigs are cooked and served whole for special occasions.

head. . . . I can see it now, lots of shredded coconut, generous pats of margarine, slices of salted egg, and a sprinkling of sugar. Yum!"[16]

For Filipinos, Christmas would not be complete without the yummy taste of bibingka. Nor would fiestas and special occasions be the same without lechon and lumpia. These delicious foods add fun to celebrations and make them more memorable.

Metric Conversions

Mass (weight)

1 ounce (oz.)	= 28.0 grams (g)
8 ounces	= 224.0 grams
1 pound (lb.) or 16 ounces	= 0.45 kilograms (kg)
2.2 pounds	= 1.0 kilogram

Liquid Volume

1 teaspoon (tsp.)	= 5.0 milliliters (ml)
1 tablespoon (tbsp.)	= 15.0 milliliters
1 fluid ounce (oz.)	= 30.0 milliliters
1 cup (c.)	= 240 milliliters
1 pint (pt.)	= 480 milliliters
1 quart (qt.)	= 0.95 liters (l)
1 gallon (gal.)	= 3.80 liters

Pan Sizes

8-inch cake pan	= 20 x 4-centimeter cake pan
9-inch cake pan	= 23 x 3.5-centimeter cake pan
11 x 7-inch baking pan	= 28 x 18-centimeter baking pan
13 x 9-inch baking pan	= 32.5 x 23-centimeter baking pan
9 x 5-inch loaf pan	= 23 x 13-centimeter loaf pan
2-quart casserole	= 2-liter casserole

Temperature

212° F	= 100° C (boiling point of water)
225° F	= 110° C
250° F	= 120° C
275° F	= 135° C
300° F	= 150° C
325° F	= 160° C
350° F	= 180° C
375° F	= 190° C
400° F	= 200° C

Length

1/4 inch (in.)	= 0.6 centimeters (cm)
1/2 inch	= 1.25 centimeters
1 inch	= 2.5 centimeters

Notes

Chapter 1: Abundant Ingredients

1. Quoted in Reynaldo G. Alejandro, *Authentic Recipes from the Philippines.* Singapore: Periplus Editions, 2005, p. 15.
2. Gilda Cordero-Fernando, *Philippine Food & Life.* Manila, Philippines: Anvil, 1992, p. 142.
3. Cordero-Fernando, *Philippine Food & Life,* p. 164.

Chapter 2: Global Tastes

4. Olivia Wu, "Laughing with Lola Cooking and Life Lessons in a Filipino Kitchen," *San Francisco Chronicle,* May 4, 2005.www.sfgate.com/cgibin/article.cgi?f=/c/ a/2005/05/04/FDGBICGTL01.DTL.
5. Gene Gonzalez, "The Little Adobo Book," Tatak Filipino. www.tatak.com/default(books)asp?cid=3& cid1 =27&pid=851.
6. Gerry Gelle, *Filipino Cuisine.* Santa Fe, NM: Red Crane, 1997, p. 136.
7. Cordero-Fernando, *Philippine Food & Life,* p. 13.

Chapter 3: Sweet Treats

8. Tribung Pinoy, "Binayong Saging." www.tribo.org/fili pinofood/recipes/binayo.html.
9. Alejandro, *Authentic Recipes from the Philippines,* p. 102.

10. Cordero-Fernando, *Philippine Food & Life,* p. 89.
11. Dianne de Las Casas, "Recipe: Leche Flan, Rich Custard from the Philippines," *The Story Connection,* May 2004. www.storyconnection.net/story_express _newsletters/StoryConnectionExpress5-5-04.pdf.

Chapter 4: Foods for Celebrations

12. Quoted in Alejandro, *Authentic Recipes from the Philippines,* p. 15.
13. Lutongbahay, "The Filipino Fiesta and the Lechon." www.lutongbahay.com/index.cfm?pagename= articles&opn=1&ArticleID=9.
14. Gelle, *Filipino Cuisine,* p. 24.
15. Gelle, *Filipino Cuisine,* p. 25.
16. Quoted in Lafang List, "Bibingka, bebinca . . . Let's call the whole thing off." http://lafang-list.bluechronicles. net/?p=42.

Glossary

adobo: A sauce made from vinegar and soy sauce.

aquaculture: Fish farming.

bagoong: A fish paste made from fermented fish or shrimp.

bangus: A popular whitefish also known as milkfish.

bibingka: A flat rice cake traditionally served at Christmas.

coconut juice: The liquid in fresh coconuts.

coconut milk: The liquid that is extracted from mature coconut meat.

flan: A sweet egg custard.

ginataan: Dishes cooked in coconut milk.

halo-halo: A tropical fruit mixture similar to fruit salad.

lechon: A roasted baby pig.

lumpia: A Filipino wrap similar to a Chinese egg roll.

merienda: Mid-morning and mid-afternoon snacks.

pancit: Noodle dishes.

patis: Fish sauce made from fermented fish or shrimp.

rice washing: The water that rice is washed in.

sabas: Small, round bananas that must be cooked before they can be eaten.

sawsawan: Dipping sauces.

sinigang: A sour soup.

water bath: A cooking method in which a small pot or cooking receptacle is placed into another pot, which contains about 1 inch (2.54cm) of hot water.

For Further Exploration

Books

Cris C. Abvia, *A Quick Guide to Filipino Food & Cooking.* Manila, Philippines: Anvil, 2001. Defines Filipino cooking terms for dishes, foods, kitchen tools, and cooking methods.

Sharon Gordon, *Philippines.* Chicago: Benchmark, 2003. Discusses the geography, people, language, and daily life in the Philippines.

Greg Nickles, *Philippines. The Culture.* New York: Crabtree, 2002. A colorful book loaded with photos, which discusses religion, arts, music, folklore, holidays and daily life in the Philippines.

World Book Staff, *Christmas in the Philippines.* Chicago: World Book Encyclopedia, 1998. Talks about the way Christmas is celebrated in the Philippines, with a chapter on food.

Web Sites

AsiaRecipe.com (http://asiarecipe.com/philippines.html). This Web site has lots of recipes, Filipino folktales, and information about Filipino culture, history, and holidays.

Learning About Each Other, (www.learnapec.org/qa/index.cfm?action=exploration&cou_id=15). Especially for kids, this Web site gives lots of facts about the Philippines with maps and photos.

Filipino Recipes (www.filipinorecipe.com). A Web site full of Filipino recipes.

Tatak Pilpino (www.tatak.com.) This is the Web site for a store in Los Angeles, California, that showcases Filipino art, music, and books. Many Filipino cookbooks and children's books are available here.

ThinkQuest (www.thinkquest.org/library/search.html). Among the different information on this site are links to information about Filipino dances, native tribes, art, sugar plantations, economic problems, and a virtual tour.

Index

adobo, 10, 19–22
Alejandro, Reynaldo, 34
aquaculture, 10
arroz caldo (souplike rice), 7–8

bagoong (fish paste), 13–14, 15
bain marie (water bath), 38
Balayan (Philippines), 44
banana cues, 30–31
bananas, 29–32, 34–36
bangus (milkfish), 10, 27
bibingka, 48, 50–51, 53, 55
breakfast foods, 7, 9
brown rice, 44

cakes, 48, 50–51, 53, 55
celebrations
  bibingka for, 48, 50–51, 53, 55
  cookware for, 49
  lechon for, 42, 44–45
  lumpia for, 46–48
champorado (porridge), 7, 9
chicken adobo, 20–22
China, 19, 22
chips, 32, 34
Christmas, 48, 50–51, 53, 55
coconuts, 7, 10, 14, 16

cookware, 21, 38, 49
Cordero-Fernando, Gilda
  on bagoong, 13–14
  on coconut milk, 16
  on halo-halo, 36
  on sinigang, 27–28

de Las Casas, Dianne, 41
desserts
  coconut, 16
  flan, 38, 41
  halo-halo, 34–36
dinner foods, 7
dips. See sauces

eating utensils, 26
egg rolls, 46–48

fast food, 39
fish, 10, 12–14, 27
flan, 38, 41
fruit
  banana, 29–32, 34–36
  sour, 27–28
  tropical, 15
  see also coconuts

garlic, 24
Gelle, Gerry, 27, 48
ginataan, 16
golden rice, 5
Gonzalez, Gene, 22

halo-halo, 34–36

inihaw cooking, 13
International Rice Institute, 9
Isidro Labrador, Saint, 52
islands, number of, 4

jackfruit, 15
John the Baptist, Saint, 44
juice, coconut, 7, 14, 16

kettles, 49
kinilaw (raw fish dishes), 10

lechons, 42, 44–45
Lukban (Philippines), 52
lumpia (egg rolls), 46–48
lunch foods, 7
Lutonbahay (Web site), 45
Luzon (Philippines), 17, 19, 52
lyaneras, 38

malagkit (sticky white rice), 5
mangos, 15
merienda, 29
Mexico, 25, 27
milagrosa (snow-white rice), 5

milk, coconut, 10, 16
milkfish, 10
Mindanao
  (Philippines), 17
Minette, 53, 55

national dish, 10, 19–22
noodles, 22–25, 27

oil, coconut, 7

pakisaw cooking, 13
pancit (noodle dish),
  22–25, 27
pastes, 13
patis (fish sauce), 13,
  27–28
pinipig, 8, 36
point-point stands, 39
pork
  for celebrations, 42,
    44–45
  on Luzon, 19
  religion and, 17
  ribs recipe, 46
purple rice, 5

queen of desserts,
  34–36

recipes
  baked bananas, 31
    bibingka, 50–51
  champorado, 9
  chicken adobo, 21
  egg noodle pancit, 23
  halo-halo, 35
  pork ribs, 46
  sinangag, 11
Reyes, Millie, 7, 42
rice, 4, 6–9, 11, 44
rice washing, 8–9, 27

sabas, 30–34
sauces
  for dipping, 13–14,
    15
  for fish, 13
  for lechon, 44–45
  for lumpia, 48
  for pancit, 25, 27
sawsawan (sauce),
  13–14
seafood, 10–14
sinangag (shrimp fried
  rice), 11
sinigang (sour soup),
  27–28
snacks

banana, 29–32, 34–36
coconut, 16
soups, 27–28
soy sauce, 10, 19
Spain
  adobo and, 19
  flan and, 38
  garlic and, 24
  pancit sauce and, 25
sugar, 29

table manners, 26
taliyasis (kettles), 49
tamarind, 15
treats. See snacks
tree of life, 7, 14
turo-turo (point-point
  stands), 39

vinegar
  in adobo, 10, 19
  cooking utensils and,
    21
  for lechon, 44
  for pakisaw, 13

water baths, 38
white rice, 5
Wu, Olivia, 20